PRESIDENT TRUMP….STOP….THE MARKET CANNOT CREATE ENOUGH JOBS….STOP: And It Is Fraudulent To Suggest It Can

By

Jim Green

DEDICATED TO [An Idea]:

THE NEIGHBOR-TO-NEIGHBOR JOB CREATION ACT [hereafter NTN, Amazon]: A federally mandated Social Insurance, held by our employed, to provide a fund to hire/train our unemployed [see hopper- ready copy of Act, Chapter 18, below]. Jobs beget jobs, and for a modest 4% of salary policy cost, we would create more "private-sector" jobs in 6 months, than HR 2847 [The HIRE ACT], in 6 years. Further, we have far more work that needs to be done in America, than persons to fill these jobs –i.e., every local jurisdiction in America would be eligible for a Grant-In-Aid—with this Act triggered by the "legal authorization" in Federal Law 15 USC § 3101—anytime our UE rate rises above 3% [i.e., at no time would we exceed 3% unemployed]. Finally, this is a Pro-Market, deficit-neutral solution [i.e., the D/UE LAW—Short Definition]: "3% is the zero-sum threshold above which unemployment starts substantially undermining the Market--and the loss in income to the Market from unemployment is compounded exponentially with each percentage point of increase in unemployment, above 3%"…..Amen

ISBN-10: 154256722X

ISBN-13: 978-1542567220

PROLOGUE

By the time this is published it will be President, rather than President-Elect Trump—but since our antiquated Electoral College tipped the election to Trump, he has been holding up the canad that if we just fix our trade agreements with other countries, we can fix our unemployment [hereafter UE] crisis...

For instance, Trump held up 700 jobs at Carrier AC, and 800 jobs at Ford, etc., as evidence of his ability to arm twist corporations to stay in America–including the threat of hefty fines after his inauguration—and he has a few takers, mostly Trump voters—who actually believe that this is solution-driven.....but when we need to create almost 200,000 jobs a month in America—just to keep up with our birthrate--it doesn't take an Einstein to figure out that tearing up trade agreements is not even any where near a solution –i.e., in fact, it is patently absurd!

Further, this mind-set dismisses the benefits we receive by these trade agreements [the anti-trade folk, which sadly also in some cases includes Bernie, want to throw the baby out with the bath water.....].

The flaw at the center of anti-trade thinking is the most pernicious belief in America, today—that: "The market can provide anybody wanting a job, with a job"—it is PURE BS—and with this propaganda/fraud driving our job creation since WW II—we have not had a UE rate below 3% since 1953! Leaving millions jobless in its wake, it has turned our inner-cities into war zones, with 60% minority UE, drug economies, and an epidemic of gun violence!

Further, when we *believe* the market can provide everybody with a job, we not only don't look at the data [which verifies it DOESN WORK]--it starts sounding reasonable to let the planet burn to the ground, so we can protect the bottom line—*every* climate-change denier believes this—and specifically because they have been taken in by this fraudulent *belief*!

Further, this stifles discussion is our search for JOBS, JOBS, JOBS—the need to look for alternatives is missed—because of the erroneous belief that we have a solution….

Lost in this discussion—Job Creation in America—is that it gets lost in ideology—and rational discussion is sabotaged when "commie" is thrown in as a monkey wrench—so real solutions don't even make it to the table!

In short, the most important issue in every election since the mid-1970's—and given "automation", alone—with growing intensity: JOBS, JOBS, JOBS—never makes it to the table…with our politicians declaring they will create "millions of jobs", if elected, but they are never asked, specifically, how they will do that! So the problem never gets solved!

The point, here, is that the solution has nothing to do with ideology—but rather turns on WHAT WORKS! It is the practicality of the situation…..The doctor can't do the operation without the proper instruments, the mechanic can't fix the engine without the proper tools—and to use a metaphor for our Job Creation in America since WW II—our Job Creation could be compared to our believing we could use a lawnmower engine in the Saturn V rocket to the Moon!

In short, skip the ideology—whether the market can, or can't fix the problem is singularly relevant to this discussion—if we are going to listen to the electorate, and FIX UNEMPLOYMENT! If what we are doing doesn't work—why do we cling to the belief that it will? In studies with mice—a mouse will stop going down a tube that doesn't have food—but not us humans—if we *believe* something—we will go down the wrong path—FOREVER—and my point is that this is the human condition that applies to this problem—and the reason we can't find a solution to our Job Creation crisis in America….IMHO…..

It all started, our being taken in by the fraud that the market can provide all the jobs we need, at the close of WW II. At the time President Truman was concerned with providing jobs for our 12 million returning troops—and the concern that if the government didn't act that it could drive us back into the Great Depression.

As a result, Truman proposed the FULL EMPLOYMENT BILL OF 1945. The Conservative/Republicans, however, went beserk—and compounded at the time by our paralysis from the Red Scare—and the birth of McCarthyism....and the Bill was watered down to suggestions, rather than having real teeth and signed into law as the EMPLOYMENT ACT OF 1945....

But the long and short is that this was the birth of the *FRAUD*, that the market can provide everybody with a job—and our Job Creation in America has been down hill ever since!

In sum....the greatest challenge facing America/Americans going forward in our 21st Century market economy is: HOW DO WE CREATE JOBS? Since WW II our Job Creation has been based on: "the market can provide anybody wanting a job, with a job"—*IT DOESN'T WORK*—but in the erroneous belief that it would--we stubbornly stood on one foot, and then the other and let Flint/Rust Belt rot into decay—and particularly egregious in that we had the "legal aurhorization" on the books at the time to prevent it—AND DID NOTHING!

And possibly in a long delayed resentment—and directed at the wrong people, and for the wrong reasons—it is probable why these folks voted for Trump......

A few closing comments in the Prologue—have decided to include some Quotes....perhaps you will like, perhaps not....but persons who commit their observations to writing, are seeking some cathartic, broad generalized truth to make the world a better place....to make sense of it all....and since FBI Director, Comey may have put the nail in the coffin for America.....written America's final chapter [i.e., the fall of the Roman Empire, etc.,....see below—an aside, WSJ had it right—Comey should resign...if he didn't understand the impact of his memo, he is too dumb to hold that job, if he did understand—his resignation is infinitely magnified!]—have decided to include those thoughts, here, my first in a Prologue....one of my favorites—as a great starting place--is from the movie The Boys In The Band..."I don't understand any of it".....

JIM GREEN QUOTES:

- If we accepted that we are animals, perhaps we could then start acting more like human beings....

- Winners want others to win....

- HAPPINESS comes from within: It is something we owe to ourselves, not something another person can give or take away....

- We have far more work that needs to be done in America, than we have persons to fill these jobs....so why in the year 2017 do we "officially" have 8 million jobless Americans—and on credible evidence, 20 million?

- The plutocracy/oligarchy in America, still has one foot on the plantation….

- The right to work and be a productive member of society, was a given in primitive societies—but lost in the Age of Industrialization—to the detriment of civilization….

- When a person is without rights –criminal wrongdoing against that person is invisible….

- The greatest enemy of capitalism is not communism or socialism---it is unemployment.

- Unemployment is a "social" problem, we as the larger society have a fiduciary obligation to address….

- The unconscionable flaw is the belief that a legal right to work is an enemy of capitalism—the fear by the plutocracy/autocracy that Humphrey-Hawkins [the most vital legislation in the 20th Century] posed a threat to special interests, rather than an adjunct…

- Re us humans, we are not as far away from being savages as we like to think we are…..

Putting Comey's unconscionable memo just before the election into context….."As nightfall does not come at once, neither does oppression. In both instances there is a twilight when everything remains seemingly unchanged. And it is in such twilight that we all must be most aware of change in the air - however slight - lest we become unwitting victims of the darkness." -William O. Douglas, former U.S. Supreme Court Justice (1898-1980)

As Oscar Wilde averred "The only truly worthless opinion is an unbiased one"—so bias, agreed—but always in the interest in getting at the larger goal—the truth….

Incidentally, I published my first book on my 78th birthday [I am currently 82]—and not that I write that fast, or well—the materials were all there for the better part of the past 30 years, give or take, gathering dust— it was just a matter of pulling them together in some order—also, don't believe any book should be over 60 pages, plus/minus— i.e., can be read in the crapper-- two hours, max--lol—but it seems best summed up by a very astute observer [wish I could recall their name to give credit]: Persons who write do so because they have no choice [it is a compulsion, an addiction..]—they become an "author", however, when people start reading what they have written….

Finally, a note to the reader—the papers and letters are not in sequence, and apologize for redundancy [please look for the nuggets…Thx--lol]—also, if you are a "typo-wonk"—are more concerned with sentence structure, etc., than content—you probably won't like my writing—and you will find a wayward capital letter, here and there, and appearing out of place and used for emphasis—or a missing page…Hey, I'm and Indie….I chalk most up to editorial license and tongue-in-cheek, self-effacing humor—so apologies, here—[I seriously support: Take what you do seriously, but never yourself….]….

Just look for content, please….THX

CHAPTER ONE

President Obama/Presidential Innovation Fellows:

Since WW II our single method of Job Creation in America has been based on the belief/propaganda that "The market can provide anybody wanting a job, with a job"......

And when it didn't work--we pretended it did, and drifted into Santa Clause-like wishful thinking— asserting "it is the American way", or "God's will"—or some such lie we told ourselves--as rational Job Creation, in a changing world, drifted further and further away.....

For instance, this method of Job Creation has not resulted in a UE rate below 3% since 1953, but we limped along—terrorized by McCarthyism, and leaving millions jobless—and by the mid-1970's the colliding forces of globalization, automation, technology reached critical mass, resulting in a cosmic shift in the world economy—with subsequent "High and persistent unemployment pervasive throughout the OECD since the mid-1970's", according to Dr. William F. Mitchell, and every credible economist.

And, going forward the data got even more grim—i.e., since 1980 we have had excessive UE 70% of the time [twice that of preceding years], and by the Crash of 2008—8 million were rendered jobless—[and in spite of an extremely anemic recovery we inched down from

10% to 5% UE, inexplicably still relying on the above method]——-

And with the result that by the September 2016 DOL Jobs Report, we still have 8 million Americans looking for work, that can't find any…..and in an economy limping along on a flat tire—as a direct result of high UE, and a Republican Congress determined to sabotage America—for political reasons--

The lesson is: Our choices are adapt and change in a world that is changing—whether we like it or not—or be forced to create a Police State to hold in place antiquated and unworkable laws and policies [in this case re our Job Creation]—and sadly, America has opted for the latter—and we need look no further than the police marching in lock-step in Charlotte, this past week, as proof!

The flaw in all of this is based on simple common sense: "The mechanic can't fix the engine without the proper tools"—and when Jobs, Jobs, Jobs is the major mantra in this election—fixing unemployment is hopeless so long as we insist on a method of Job Creation—THAT DOESN'T WORK!

Proposed Solutions: HR 1000, and FULL EMPLOYMENT IS A PRO-MARKET CONCEPT, Amazon

Jim Green, Democrat opponent to Lamar Smith, 2000

Thank you for contacting the White House!

CHAPTER TWO

President Obama/Council of Economic Advisers:

Capitalism is ideal in producing and selling corn flakes and cars—It doesn't work in solving "social problems" such as unemployment and our healthcare....

And when we have tried "privatization" to solve our social problems—it has been a disaster:

Specifically, essential programs have been cut—such as the elimination of text books from the Job Corps education program—to increase profits, and cronyism has run rampant—

And in our "for profit" healthcare system, billions of dollars are siphoned away from the premiums we send in—and do not go to the healthcare of ANYONE—but rather is used to pay for lobbyists, to make the CEO's filthy rich—and spent on propaganda ads to keep it that way!

Additionally, President Obama had a weapon in 2009, not available to FDR: Were it not for the $800 billion in Social Security Insurance moneys percolating up through our economy annually, ie., in 2008—we would

not be talking about having narrowly averted another Great Depression—We would be buried in one!

The truth is, we have a blended economic system—and the two components are, in fact, indispensable to each other:

Social Insurance is a vital ingredient in building a vibrant and decent society—And, invent a better widget, sell the company for a million bucks, and retire in Florida [capitalism]—is as well a vital ingredient in building a vibrant and decent society.

So why do we have this war of words pitting the two against each other—rather than educating the American people regarding the indispensable symbiotic relationship they have to each other?

Were it not for the $2 trillion + Washington infuses back into the economy annually—capitalism would fold in a NY Second!

And yet, most Republicans ask God in their prayers at night to be protected from communists, or socialists, or even worse "liberals"—[i.e., monsters under their bed] with "liberal" henceforth to be replaced with the word "Christian"…..

Regarding "unemployment" [hereafter UE]—it is essential that we evolve, and given "automation", alone, in our 21st Century economy we need to look upon UE the same as we look upon Cancer, Polio, or AIDS, as a ubiquious disease—a menace to society, in need of eradication….via [15 USC § 3101]—which would restrict our UE to 3%, permanently!

Re: IT IS IMPOSSIBLE TO BE A CHRISTIAN, AND VOTE REPUBLICAN, Amazon/Kindle

Jim Green, Democrat opponent to Lamar Smith, 2000

Thank you for contacting President Obama.

CHAPTER THREE

President Obama/Council of Economic Advisers:

Every credible economist agrees that "High and persistent unemployment has pervaded almost every OECD country since the mid-1970's"....and almost 1 in 2 Americans [43%] cite Job Creation as the Number One issue in the 2016 election....

And yet, addressing the devastating results of unemployment [hereafter UE], as a stand-alone problem, to be solved the same as we would look upon a pandemic, is not in any of the debates, and while all of our candidates say they will create JOBS, our current solution to UE is analogous to not putting gas in our car, and then puzzling over why it doesnl't run.....and we need look no further than Flint, to understand the devastating results of UE.....

For instance, since WW II, the American people have been sold a Bill of Goods that "the market can provide anybody wanting a job, with a job"—which the data shows to be pure BS....and only ONCE since WW II has this Job Creation methodology resulted in a UE rate below 3%--in 1953—leaving millions jobless in its wake—and resulting in our inner-cities becoming war zones, with an epidemic of gun violence.....

And while all of the candidates talk about how they will create jobs, the REAL issue--the adverse consequences of unemployment —both to the jobless and the market…never gets discussed…..i.e., UE is a NO ONE WINS…the jobless lose, civility loses [Ferguson, etc.], and the market loses, to wit:

THE LAW OF DIMINISHED INCOME TO THE MARKET FROM UNEMPLOYMENT [hereafter D/UE LAW]

> 3% is the zero-sum threshold above which unemployment triggers inflation by diminishing labor training and skills, under-utilizing capital resources, reducing the rate of productivity advance, increasing unit labor costs, reducing the general supply of goods and services--and the loss in income to the Market is compounded exponentially with each percentage point of increase in unemployment, above 3%.

Finally, it would be ideal if the market could provide all of the jobs we need—but pretending that the market can provide a solution it is INCAPABLE of providing is analogous to our putting a lawnmower engine in the Saturn V rocket to the Moon…..

Ref: HR 1000 [in Committee]; THE NEIGHBOR-TO-NEIGHBOR JOB CREATION ACT, and FULL EMPLOYMENT IS A PRO-MARKET CONCEPT, Amazon, Kindle

Jim Green, Democrat opponent to Lamar Smith, Congress, 2000

CC: Donald Trump

CHAPTER FOUR

To The Honorable President Obama:

HR 1000 [In Committee] IS INDISPENSABLE IN OUR WINNING THE WAR AGAINST TERRORISM

This letter is to urge you to award the Presidential Medal of Freedom to U.S. Representative John Conyers, from Michigan.

Not only is he the longest-serving member of Congress—he has tirelessly worked for the Full Employment of Americans [HR 1000, in Committee], and in addressing inequity in America—a Renaissance Man in our 21st Century economy, who was present in Selma, on Freedom Day, October 7, 1963.

Further, Representative Conyers has made "an especially meritorious contribution to the security or national interests of the United States, world peace, cultural or other significant public or private endeavors" [the purpose for this award].

Few Americans are more deserving.

Finally, his appointment will call attention to the most important legislation in the 20th Century in our War On Terrorism, and indispensable to the effective functioning of our 21st Century market economy—pro-market Humphrey-Hawkins Full Employment Act, signed into law by President Carter [15 USC § 3101]. We have had excessive unemployment 70% of the time since 1980 as a result of automation/globalization, alone, and the implementation of this law [integral to HR 1000] will address the number one issue in the 2016 election: Jobs in our 21st Century market economy.

Ref: FULL EMPLOYMENT IS A PRO-MARKET CONCEPT, Amazon/Kindle

With highest regards,

Jim Green, Democrat candidate for Congress, District 21, TX, 2000

Thank you for contacting the White House!

CHAPTER FIVE

President Obama/Council of Economic Advisers:

"The truth is poetry, problem is—most people hate poetry" Mark Twain

What if you knew something that would eradicate terrorism...but because of tradition, resistance to change, etc., your information is not readily understood....but at the risk of being stereotyped by the GE ad, and for the sake of discussion—here goes:

First, it needs to be understood that the most dangerous belief afoot in America today, is "the market can provide anybody wanting a job, with a job"—and while every Republican in Congress believes it to be true—it is dangerous, because it is PURE BS......

Indeed, so prevalent is this belief that it has dominated our Job Creation since WW II—and in spite of the fact that this has resulted in an unemployment [hereafter UE] rate below 3% only ONCE since WW II—in 1953—leaving millions jobless in its wake since, and has resulted in 60% minority UE in our inner-cities, drug economies, and an epidemic of gun violence—

Also, with the proliferation of automation, alone, in the mid-1970's, and subsequent loss of employment, we have had excessive UE 70% of the time in the U.S., since 1980—

Further, as a result of the paradigm shift in the 1970's, UE is accelerating the further we advance into the 21st Century....i.e., with 10% UE now common in the Eurozone--25% in Greece and Spain....and UE was a major factor in Arab Spring....

And here is where common sense comes in.....we need look no further than Flint, to understand the devastating results of UE, and statistics show that with each point of increase in the UE rate, 40,000 die in ancillary damage!

And yet, in spite of the damage, we have yet to identify UE as a "social" problem, ever bit as damaging as a pandemic—i.e., WE, as the larger society, have a solemn responsibility to address...but which we ignore with the rationalization that "No sweat, the market has this covered"....and Flint is the result.....

Finally, in this dynamic, the right to work and be a productive member of society was a given in primitive societies—but lost in the Age of Industrialization--and the indifference by the larger society to the importance of employment [inclusion], has become a breeding ground for terrorism.....

Ref: HR 1000 [in Committee], ECONOMIC INCLUSIVISM, and FULL EMPLOYENT IS A PRO-MARKET CONCEPT, Amazon/Kindle

Jim Green, Democrat opponent to Lamar Smith, 2000

Thank you for contacting the White House!

CHAPTER SIX

President Obama/Council of Economic Advisers:

Our current method of Job Creation in America is a miserable failure—our proof is the fact that the number one issue in the 2016 election is JOBS—and we have had excessively high unemployment [hereafter UE] 70% of the time since 1980—[double that in prior years] with automation, alone, accelerating our UE the further we advance into the 21st Century.....

In truth, the world has changed and our UE crisis, with 20 million jobless Americans, is mired in the 18th Century as a result of Job Creation policies which have one foot on the plantation---in a 21st Century market economy--

Since WW II the oligarchy has spent tens of millions [buying elections/politicians] to look the other way, and turn their back on the will of the American people— i.e., and let the oligarchy write our Job Creation policy in America—it is based on the propaganda/lie that "the market can provide anybody wanting a job, with a job"—which the data shows to be Pure BS—

That is, only ONCE since WW II has this method of Job Creation resulted in a UE rate below 3%--in 1953—leaving millions jobless in its wake, and has resulted in 60% minority UE in our inner-cities, drug economies, and an epidemic of gun violence!

We need look no further than Flint to understand the destructive effects of unemployment--and WE are a "can do" nation—but when it comes to our Job Creation in America, our policies could be compared to our scientists putting a lawnmower engine in the Saturn 5 Rocket to the Moon.....

And the over-arching question, today, is: When our method of job creation doesn't work....why on God's earth do we continue down this path? And, particularly given the pervasive damage caused by UE--This criticism is not anti-capitalism—it is a statement of fact!

And ignored in all of this is that "We have far more work that needs to be done in America, than we have persons to fill these jobs", and "86% of Americans believe that anybody wanting to work should be able to find a job".....UE is a NO ONE WINS: The jobless lose, civility loses [Ferguson, etc.,].....

And, the Market loses!

INDISPENSABLE to the EFFECTIVE functioning of our market economy going forward in the 21st Century is: HR 1000 [in Committee], and/or THE NEIGHBOR-TO-NEIGHBOR JOB CREATION ACT, Amazon/Kindle—or like Job Creation....

Jim Green, Democrat opponent to Lamar Smith, 2000

CHAPTER SEVEN

This is an election year, why is this being ignored by the media?

President Obama/Council of Economic Advisers:

We need look no further than Flint to understand the destructive effects of unemployment [hereafter UE]----as destructive to a community as a pandemic—

And yet, we—as the larger society—are prepared to pool all of our resources to eradicate a pandemic with all deliberate speed—but we turned our back and run the other way from the destruction to Flint—i.e., we allowed Flint to fall into decay as a result of UE—indeed, we have a "Rust Belt" in America, because of the same phenomenon.

Problem is, Washington pretends all of this is normal—A position not shared by the tens of thousands that are showing up to protest at rallies--for Sanders and Trump....

Michael Moore has documented the destruction of Flint in "Roger and Me"—which went from a thriving community of 80,000, with little crime, in the 1970's—to 50,000 by 1990, with 60% minority UE, the highest violent crime rate in America, and an epidemic of gun violence....

And while the focus by Moore was on the "unjustified" plant closings by GM--it was a missed opportunity to focus on UE as a "social" problem we as the larger society have a fiduciary obligation to address......

After all, we should never condemn a CEO who closes a plant because they are losing money [which Moore asserts did not apply to GM]—but we are outraged by a government that is indifferent to finding a solution.

And the irony is that in 1978 [perfect timing to rescue Flint], President Carter signed into law a "legal authorization" to restrict our UE rate to "3%" permanently [15 USC § 3101]—i.e., at no time, and to this day, should the UE rate in Flint, or anywhere else in America, exceed 3%--so why, and to this day, does Washington pretend this law doesn't exist?

The answer underscores the criminality in Citizens United—and the hundreds of millions spent buying our elections since WW II, and the warning from the 1% to bought and paid for politicians: Noli Tangere [do not touch] Job Creation in America—the result has been a disaster, and only ONCE since WW II has 1% Job Creation resulted in a UE rate below 3%--in 1953--- leaving millions jobless in its wake, and our inner-cities a mirror image of Flint!

Ref: HR 1000 [in Committee]; THE CASE FOR WORK BEING A LEGAL RIGHT, and FULL EMPLOYMENT IS A PRO-MRKET CONCEPT, Amazon/Kindle

Jim Green, Democrat opponent to Lamar Smith, 2000

Thank you for contacting the White House!

CHAPTER EIGHT

President Obama:

When you took office it appeared—finally, and with a Democrat house and senate—that we would finally fix unemployment [hereafter UE] in America.

And particularly since the mantra, and getting louder in every election since 1980, has been FIX UNEMPLOYMENT. In fact, we have had excessive UE 70% of the time since 1980 [double that of preceding years].

According to Dr. William F. Mitchell, and every credible economist, "High and persistent unemployment has pervaded almost every OECD country since the mid-1970's".

And in 1978, the U.S. took a proactive step by providing a "legal authorization" to end our unemployment crisis [15 USC § 3101], and least understood is that implementation of this law is Pro-Market—i.e., given automation, alone, our taking this step is INDISPENSABLE to the EFFECTIVE functioning of our 21st Century market economy.

Since WW II the archaic model we have been operating under [and bought and paid for in our elections by the plutocracy/oligarchy] is "fix the market, and this will fix unemployment", rather than "fix unemployment and this will fix the market"—

And running in parallel is the most pernicious propaganda in America, today, i.e., that "the market can provide anybody wanting a job, with a job"—it is pure BS—and only ONCE since WW II has this Job Creation model resulted in a UE rate below 3%--in 1953—leaving millions jobless in its wake, and leaving our inner-cities with 60% minority UE, drug economies, and an epidemic of gun violence!

In any event, when we Democrats failed to fix UE, a retaliatory electorate filled the House with lunatics in the 2010 election, and DC has been in paralysis ever since…...and also accounts for the masses showing up at Sanders/Trump rallies….

For clarity of the above…Humphrey-Hawkins is brilliant, ahead of its time—more valuable with each passing year—and incredibly misunderstood…….i.e., had Carter enforced the "legal authorization" in this law, he signed--and, in fact, reduced our UE rate to "3%" as provided for in the law—there is no way he would have lost the election to Reagan…….

Deficit-Neutral Solutions: HR 1000 [in Committee]; THE NEIGHBOR-TO-NEIGHBOR JOB CREATION ACT, and THE CASE FOR WORK BEING A LEGAL RIGHT, Amazon/Kindle

Jim Green, Democrat opponent to Lamar Smith, 2000 Bio: http://www.amazon.com/James-L.-Jim-Green/e/B001KHZIMM/ref=ntt_dp_epwbk_0

Thank you for contacting the White House!

CHAPTER NINE

President Obama/Council of Economic Advisers:

We do not currently have a legal right to work because we are living in the dark ages—in denial re automation, alone, in our 21st Century market economy--to the detriment of the market!

In fact, we have had excessive unemployment [hereafter UE] 70% of the time since 1980 [twice that of preceding years] as the result of a paradigm shift, an adjustment towards modernity, in the world economy in the mid-1970's—resulting from the colliding forces of globalization, automation, technology, etc., reaching critical mass.

Indeed, the U.S. responded directly to this paradigm shift with Pro-Market landmark legislation in 1978 [15 USC § 3101], to lawfully limit our UE rate in America to 3% permanently, henceforth—but in a desperate effort to cling to the past and maintain the status quo, the Koch brothers [a metaphor, here, for the 1%] bought off Washington via our elections—to prevent this law from ever taking effect…..

It is akin to the adage that world travel was out of the question when consensus had it that the world was flat….and we have paid a terrible price by our unwillingness to evolve: The loss of our manufacturing base, a weak recovery, and Trump as a candidate for president [i.e., his magical thinking /angry

constituency—i.e, with some overlap with Bernie]….it is a recipe for disaster!

Indeed, the over-flow crowds showing up at Bernie's rallies—and perhaps while not framed in the same words….is a protest against Washington for not making work a legal right—i.e., a protest against DC for clinging to the status quo, rather than evolving so that America will be in line with the 21st Century.

The bottom line is that UE is a NO ONE WINS: The jobless lose, civility loses [Ferguson, etc.], and the Market loses, to wit:

THE LAW OF DIMINISHED INCOME TO THE MARKET FROM UNEMPLOYMENT [hereafter D/UE LAW]

Short Definition:

> 3% is the zero-sum threshold above which unemployment starts substantially undermining the Market--and the loss in income to the Market is compounded exponentially with each percentage point of increase in unemployment, above 3%.

Ref: HR 1000 [in Committee]; FULL EMPLOYMENT IS A PRO-MARKET CONCEPT, and THE CASE FOR WORK BEING A LEGAL RIGHT, Amazon/Kindle

Jim Green, Democrat opponent to Lamar Smith, Congress, 2000

Thank you for contacting the White House!

CHAPTER TEN

President Obama/Council of Economic Advisers:

95% OF OUR SOCIAL ILLS WILL DISAPPEAR TOMORROW BY GETTING OUR FACTS AND PRIORITIES STRAIGHT….

We need look no further than Flint to readily see the devastation and injury to humans from unemployment [hereafter UE]—and documented in "Roger and Me". So why are we silent on the devastation to the Market, caused by UE? People do not buy what we manufacture when they are jobless….but whenever we talk about the evaporation of our manufacturing base….we blame outsourcing….rather than placing the blame where it most belongs—on our Job Creation incompetence! And fueled by the false and unworkable belief that "the market can provide anybody wanting a job, with a job." It is Pure BS…not supported by the data, and with a miserable record of Job Creation! And yet, it has been our sole Job Creation methodology since WW II….and via its incompetence, it has turned our inner-cities into war zones with an epidemic of gun violence….and a Rust Belt as Exhibit One!

The truth is: Unemployment is a NO ONE WINS….the jobless lose, civility loses [Ferguson, etc.,], and the Market loses, to wit:

THE LAW OF DIMINISHED INCOME TO THE MARKET FROM UNEMPLOYMENT [hereafter D/UE LAW]

Short Definition:

3% is the zero-sum threshold above which
unemployment starts substantially undermining
the Market--and the loss in income to the Market
is compounded exponentially with each
percentage point of increase in unemployment,
above 3%.

Ref: HR 1000 [in Committee], THE CASE FOR
WORK BEING A LEGAL RIGHT: Our Only Path To
Prison Reform, and, FULL EMPLOYMENT IS A
PRO-MARKET CONCEPT, Amazon/Kindle

Jim Green, Democrat opponent to Lamar Smith,
Congress, 2000

CHAPTER ELEVEN

President Obama/Council of Economic advisers:

73% of Americans have expressed a generalized anger—but when pinned down they cannot give a specific reason.....mostly it is expressed as a feeling—and centers around the economy and jobs—and is most often stated as "We are moving in the wrong direction".....

The purpose of this letter is to brazenly offer an explanation—IMHO—and would bet the farm I have it on the nose....

For instance, both the Democrats and Republicans miss it by making "minimum wage" the issue in this election—rather than making "work", itself, the issue—and admittedly Republicans/Trump refer to the former dragging both feet—but this evening Trump grudgingly agreed on a $10 minimum wage, on O'Reilly—but no one is taking stock that a minimum wage is meaningless to a person who is jobless!

And as Trump rightly noted—the "official" jobless number of 8 million is a joke—i.e., with the DOL not counting persons who have given up—the true number is closer to 20 million unemployed Americans! And, we need look no further than Flint to understand the devastation caused by unemployment, and yet neither party is citing the CAUSE, in search of a solution!

That is, that we have a phony/baloney method of Job Creation in America—to use street language—and yet, Washington keeps perpetuating the lie that the market can provide all the jobs we need—it is PURE BS!

Further, the right to work and be productive member of society was a given in primitive societies, but lost in the Age of Industrialization—

It is a fact that a "do nothing" Republican Congress has Washington ground to a halt—to the detriment of America—but another factor, never discussed, is that a Washington that has been bought and paid for by Special Interests—is deaf, dumb and blind when it comes to finding a solution to our antiquated method of Job Creation!

But rather than admitting this—and sitting down at the table to find real solutions….Washington tries to paper over it, and/or pretend it doesn't exist….

We have the solution—we have the "legal authorization" on the books, to limit our UE to 3%--permanently—and pending legislation in Congress: HR 1000—So WHY is this not the NUMBER ONE issue in this election?

Ref: FULL EMPLOYMENT IS A PRO-MARKET CONCEPT, Amazon/Kindle

Jim Green, Democrat candidate for Congress, 2000

PS Apologize for CAPS—your software doesn't allow emphasis….

CHAPTER TWELVE

President Obama/Council of Economic Advisers:

THE HISTORY OF HUMPHREY-HAWKINS

The historic March On Washington, and Dr. King's "I had a dream" speech, in 1963, was a march for JOBS.

At that time, and to this day, our job creation in America has been based on the premise that "the market can provide anybody wanting a job, with a job—

And yet, only ONCE since WW II has this method of job creation resulted in an unemployment rate below 3%--in 1953—leaving millions jobless in its wake.

Following Dr. Kings death in 1968, civil rights leaders, including Jesse Jackson, annually marched on Dr. King's birthday for legislation that would address our pervasive unemployment in America.

Their demand was not without legal foundation. In 1946, President Truman signed into law the [FULL] EMPLOYMENT ACT OF 1946, to provide employment for our troops returning from WW II.

The 1%, however, balked at American employees having rights—particularly a right to employment [the model which exists to this day]—and the law was never implemented.

Ironically, Australia enacted a law similar to President Truman's Employment Act—and for the same reason—and for the next 30 years [and until the ill-winds of neo-liberalism in the mid-1970's] Australia's employment model was based on the premise that "anybody wanting to work should be able to find a job"—with 2% or less unemployment common. Australians still refer to this as their "Golden Age".

As a result of the demand by civil rights leaders for legislation, however, in 1978 President Carter signed into law—what is commonly known as the Humphrey-Hawkins Full Employment Act [15 USC § 3101].

The law provides the "legal authorization" for the creation of a "reservoir of public employees" anytime our unemployment in America exceeds "3%". That is, and to this day—at no time should our unemployment rate in America exceed 3%.

The money in politics, however, has prevented this law from being implemented!

Notwithstanding, a lone Congressman, Conyers [and a growing number of co-sponsors] has diligently worked to implement Humphrey-Hawkins [currently, deficit-neutral HR 1000, in Committee].

And, singularly, unemployment is the most pernicious problem facing America, today....

Ref: FULL EMPLOYMENT IS A PRO-MARKET CONCEPT, Amazon

Jim Green, Democrat opponent to Lamar Smith, 2000

Thank You!

Thank you for contacting the White House.

CHAPTER THIRTEEN

President Obama:

It is impossible to reform our broken criminal justice system—absent our creating a viable job creation program in America.

And while it is generally believed that we do have a job creation program, in fact, we do not!

We have the BELIEF that "the market can provide anybody wanting a job, with a job"—but the data shows that only ONCE since WW II has this belief resulted in an unemployment rate below 3%--in 1953—leaving millions jobless in its wake-- and has resulted in:

60% minority unemployment in our inner-cities, with drug economies, and an epidemic of homicides [i.e., not fixing unemployment has turned our inner-cities into war zones, and created a breeding ground for our inexplicable incarceration rate].

Further this "belief" has been a stumbling block in finding a solution for our pervasive unemployment--In short, we have not been looking for a solution—because our policy makers believe we have one—and apparently few have looked at the data....

Also, ignored in the discussion is that unemployment is a "social" problem, with adverse, and oft severe social consequences—both for the individual, as well as the larger society [i.e., it is the responsibility of the larger society to solve]—

With tentacles integral to all of the social problems facing Americans, today—for instance, ending unemployment is integral to Criminal Justice Reform, and the repair of our crumbling infrastructure....

Further, in 1975 we spent $5 educating our youth, for every $1 we spent on prisons.....by the mid-1990's [with the American people having been terrorized by the Willie Horton ad—and on an hysterical prison building spree] our competing tax dollars tipped in favor of prisons—and at present we spend more on prisons, than on educating our youth.

The irony in all of this is that we have the "legal authorization", on the books to reduce our unemployment rate to 3%, tomorrow [15 USC § 3101—and deficit-neutral HR 1000, currently in Committee]—and also ignored in this context, is that President Obama had a weapon in addressing our economic meltdown in 2008, not available to FDR—and that is the $800 billion in Social Security Insurance claims percolating up through our economy—and in the absence of which--We would be buried in another Great Depression!

Turning the page—and given "automation", alone, is critical going forward in the 21st Century—and is a "win-win"—the American people win, and the market wins....

Ref: FULL EMPLOYMENT IS A PRO-MARKET CONCEPT, Amazon

Jim Green, Democrat opponent to Lamar Smith, 2000

CHAPTER FOURTEEN

President Obama/Council of Economic Advisers:

Our network of market-driven economies [the OECD, including the U.S]—currently have a pernicious job creation modality—with resulting high and pervasive unemployment since the mid-1970's—and on a collision course with the future—i.e., given "automation", alone, fewer and fewer jobs are being created with each passing year, as we advance into the 21st Century....

This job creation modality is based on the erroneous propaganda/belief that "the market can provide anybody wanting a job, with a job"—and yet, only ONCE since WW II has this modality resulted in an unemployment rate below 3%--in 1953—leaving millions jobless in its wake, and has resulted in our inner-cities turning into war zones--with 60% minority unemployment, drug economies, and an epidemic of homicides.

The irony in this disaster, however, is that the U.S. correctly anticipated this result in 1978—and provided the American people with a solution, i.e., the "legal authorization" [15 USC § 3101] to limit our unemployment henceforth to "3%", and as we advance into the 21st Century—

With a ton of cash poured into our political system, and a mind-set with both feet planted on the plantation—-- special interests sabotaged this law to prevent its

implementation—to the detriment of Americans, and America [ISIS is the least of our worries in America, when we have the Republican party]!

Unemployment is a "social" problem, with adverse social consequences....it is solely the province of the larger society to solve—and leaving the solution to anything as erratic as the market—as we do now—is patently absurd!

The bottom line is that unemployment is a **NO ONE WINS**....the jobless lose, civility loses, and the market loses, to wit:

THE LAW OF DIMINISHED INCOME TO THE MARKET FROM UNEMPLOYMENT [hereafter D/UE LAW]

3% is the zero-sum threshold above which unemployment triggers inflation by diminishing labor training and skills, under-utilizing capital resources, reducing the rate of productivity advance, increasing unit labor costs, reducing the general supply of goods and services--and the loss in income to the Market is compounded exponentially with each percentage point of increase in unemployment, above 3%.

Ref: HR 1000 [in Committee], and FULL EMPLOYMENT IS A PRO-MARKET SOLUTION, Amazon

Jim Green, Democrat opponent to Lamar Smith, 2000

Thank You!

Thank you for contacting the White House

CHPATER FIFTEEN

THE HISTORY OF HOW WE GOT WHERE WE ARE
[WW II to Present]

Following WW II, President Truman signed into law the [FULL] EMPLOYMENT ACT of 1946, to provide employment for our returning troops.

Ironically, half-way around the world, Australia codified into their law an almost identical Bill, and for the same reason—

Difference is—Australia actually put their law into effect, and over the next 30 years it was intrinsic to employment policy in Australia that "anybody wanting to work should be able to find a job"—and save for a brief recession in 1961/62 their unemployment was 2%, or less. This period is still referred to as their "Golden Age", in Australia.

Unforeseen by either country, however, in the mid-1970's the world economy underwent a major paradigm shift as a result of the colliding forces of automation, globalization, technology, etc., reaching a critical mass—in brief, an adjustment towards modernity—From a perverse perspective, we became victims of our success....

The instability caused by this transition, however, resulted in a malaise, and ushered in the ill-winds of greed-driven neo-liberalism with its indifference to unemployment, and the likes of Thatcher and Reagan—and the menace of this greed-driven agenda was exploded by Bush II, resulting in obscene disparities in wealth that persists, and is the cause of much friction between right and left, to this day.

It also ushered in high and pervasive unemployment throughout our market-driven economies, the OECD—with 6% unemployment in Australia now the norm, and double-digit unemployment common throughout the Eurozone, to this day.

As a result of the "malaise", however, the U.S. took an aggressive, pro-active role in addressing the, above, economic shift—and in 1978 President Carter signed into law one of the most important laws in the 20th Century--an expansion of President Truman's full employment, i.e., Pro-Market 15 USC § 3101--which provides a "*legal authorization*" to create a "reservoir of public employees" [*indispensable to the effective functioning of a 21st Century market economy*]--at any time our unemployment in America exceeds "3%"—

But in spite of 3% unemployment being the threshold point above which unemployment starts substantially undermining the Market—this *legal authorization* has never been implemented--

And in spite of deficit-neutral HR 1000, or The Neighbor-To-Neighbor Job Creation Act—A federally mandated Social Insurance, owned by our employed, to provide a fund to hire/train our unemployed—[more on the critical need to apply this job creation methodology in a 21st Century market economy, ahead]….

Ref: FULL EMPLOYMENT IS A PRO-MARKET CONCEPT, Amazon/Kindle

Jim Green, Democrat opponent to Lamar Smith, Congress, 2000

CHAPTER SIXTEEN

THE HISTORY OF HOW WE GOT WHERE WE ARE

[Mid-1970's to Present]

In the mid-1970's, the colliding forces of automation, technology, globalization, etc., reached a critical mass—resulting in a Market no longer capable of producing the jobs necessary to its viability, and causing ubiquitous unemployment in all of the OECD countries—and leaving their leaders conflicted, ever since, regarding the displaced employee. Eurozone unemployment is still in double digits, and Greece and Spain both in excess of 20%, plus. High unemployment was also a major factor in Arab Spring.

In the U.S., we took a pro-active role in addressing this economic shift—and in 1978 President Carter signed into law 15 USC § 3101--which "authorizes" the creation of a "reservoir of public employment" at any time our unemployment in America exceeds "3%".

In 1979, however, and in a panic over Humphrey-Hawkins—our ultra-conservative foundations, and desperate to promote the Supply-Side fraud, embraced a flawed paper by an obscure MIT student, David L. Birch "The Job Generation Process"; and [with lots of cash] gave his paper biblical importance, and every president since has cited his finding as gospel.

Birch's paper concluded that "small businesses" were the greatest generator of new jobs—problem is, for the purposes of policy-making—it is BS. In a study at Harvard University in 2010, "The Myth of Small Business Job Creation" The research shows "no systematic relationship between firm size and growth." And that small businesses can actually detract from job growth.

In spite of this, however, Washington struggles, still, to make this antiquated notion, work--that it is only the market that can create jobs—and the result has been a disaster, politically as well as otherwise!

It would be impossible to still have 7.8% unemployment—if we were on the right path—and among other problems with this concept--if the market fails, the unemployed are out of luck.

Further, unemployment is a "social" problem we are seeking to address with a highly unstable, incompatible entity: The Market

What apparently isn't clear going forward is that an expanding and contracting public workforce is an *indispensable* component to the *effective* functioning of a modern market economy—

The market thrives when we have a robust, employed, consuming workforce—and overlooked is that HR 1000 [currently in Committee], and the proposed "Neighbor-To-Neighbor Job Creation Act" www.Inclusivism.org [both authorized under Humphrey-Hawkins], are deficit-neutral--Pro-Market "win-win" solutions:

The American people win, and capitalism wins—

Jim Green, Democrat candidate for Congress, 2000

CHAPTER SEVENTEEN

Friends: In the event you have gotten this far—according to the Federal Election Commission, I am a candidate for president in the 2016 election—and rest assured I am not delusional, or like Trump…on an ego trip…..I filed solely to deliver a message—you are reading it—and to urge passage of the above legislation….

To Whom It May Concern—in Washingon:

OUR CHOICES ARE: Adapt and change in a world that is changing, whether we like it or not, OR be forced to create a Police State to hold our anachronistic policies, practices and laws in place—

And in America, today, we have chosen the latter…..and as only one pernicious example, of thousands—Ferguson is the result….

In a comedic, but religious context we hear of persons asking God for a sign—anything—which will warn us that we are on the wrong path, and need to change direction…..and our Police State choice, above, is *our sign*…..few are listening….

To illustrate a critical area in which we need to adapt and change in a 21st Century economy: We have far more work that needs to be done in America, than we have persons to fill these jobs—And 86% of Americans believe that "Anybody wanting to work should be able to find a job"---So, why on earth *in a democracy*, do we have 9 million jobless Americans—[per the 11/14 DOL Jobs report]?

The answer is because our *method* of job creation in America is based on a Fairy Tale! Specifically, our current *one and only* job creation methodology in America, is based on the myth/sacred cow:

"The market can provide anybody wanting a job, with a job"—

Problem is—it is pure BS—and only *once* since WW II has this methodology resulted in an unemployment rate below 3%--in 1953 [i.e., which translates into 5 million left jobless]--because the market *cannot* create enough jobs—in short, the jobs for this 5 million jobless--*don't exist*!

The right-wing propaganda mills trick our fools into believing that the market has created this 5 million jobs, but because those on welfare are "lazy and don't want to work" this 5 million jobs go unfilled—but that is *pure balderdash!*

The vast majority of persons on welfare, are there *because* the *market* cannot create enough jobs, i.e., the market lacks the viability to create these jobs—the jobs simply *do not exist*!

And as further proof, according to the CBO, on our current path it will be 2017 before America returns to even an anemic 5.5% unemployment rate [following the Great Recession] and if the market fails in the interim—the jobless are out of luck!

Further, this travesty is compounded because the Republicans cling to devious and discredited Supply Side Economics [to this day] as a solution, to wit:

Siphon America's wealth away from the consuming middle—give this windfall of cash to the Koch Bros [a metaphor for the 1%, hereafter "KB"]—they will build factories all across our fair land—everyone will have a job in the corporation—and we will all live happily ever after—Yes, folks it is a fairy tale!

And what we learned from this dark cloud over America is what Bush I called it long ago—before America was subjected to this devious scam—i.e., Supply-Side is "VooDoo Economics"!

So why have we allowed ourselves to be deceived by this Republican scam—[handcrafted by a plutocracy/oligarchy that still has one foot on the plantation]? But I don't want to giveaway the surprise ending—and some of my response isn't printable....! Further, and to say it up front....I am a capitalist—I support 100%: Build a better widget, sell it for a million bucks, and retire in South Florida....it is the Republican agenda, today, that is anti-market...more on this throughout.....

When President Carter handed the reigns over to Reagan in 1981—he left America with a very modest

$60 billion deficit—as a direct result of Supply-Side, however, when Republicans held the White House [Clinton actually cut the deficit]—this $60 billion ballooned to a staggering $10 trillion by 2008—and it has cost Americans an additional $7+trillion to clean up this Republican mess—

Ask any economist: Our only way out of a meltdown *is to buy our way out!* [it was the lesson learned from the Great Depression].

And anyone who thinks McCain, had he been elected, would not have addressed this with a Stimulus, the same as President Obama in 2009—is stuffed between the ears with rice pudding......

Further, we learned that we cannot siphon America's wealth away from the consuming middle, and give it to the "KB"—without sending our economy into meltdown—as occurred in 1987 and 2008—in short, the Supply-Side scam has a shelf-life of about 7 years before the economy collapses—and as noted, costing the taxpayers trillions to put a floor under a disappearing economy!

And another fallout/direct result from this dark chapter is the disparity in wealth it has created in America—AKA the "wealth gap"--and currently the "richest 1 percent in the United States now own more wealth than the bottom 90 percent"—the second highest in our history, the first was just before the Great Depression.

A couple of other factors that played into the above scenario—when every waking moment in capitalism is spent pondering how to eliminate as many of us humans, as possible, from the workplace—to increase "profits"—why, on Earth, would we look to the market to solve our unemployment crisis in America?

As well, few things on earth are more unstable than the market….we can count on one hand the number of corporations in America that were around in 1900….with tens of thousands long since disappeared; and given "automation", alone, the market will produce fewer and fewer jobs the further we advance into the 21st Century.

Further, unemployment is a "social" problem—we, as the larger society have the responsibility to solve—i.e., it is unrealistic to expect the market to solve this problem—the market is in the "for profit" business, not the social work business—and the former would not long be in business--if they were…for example, we should never condemn the CEO for closing a plant when they are losing money—but we should be outraged by a government that doesn't have a clue re the displaced employees…..

Also, unemployment is a _no one wins_ …..the jobless lose, and market loses, to wit:

> 3% is the zero-sum threshold above which unemployment triggers inflation by diminishing labor training and skills, under-utilizing capital resources, reducing the rate of productivity

advance, increasing unit labor costs, and reducing the general supply of goods and services--and the loss in income to the Market is compounded exponentially with each percentage point of increase in unemployment, above 3%.

Short Definition:

3% is the zero-sum threshold above which unemployment starts substantially undermining the Market--and the loss in income to the Market is compounded exponentially with each percentage point of increase in unemployment, above 3%.

In sum, our job creation should be based on: Fix unemployment, and this will fix the market [HR 1000], rather than [our current mind-set] Fix the market, and this in turn fix unemployment [HR 2847] – with a result that has been a disaster—as we inch along in our job recovery, see data above, and when we didn't *Fix Unemployment* a retaliatory electorate ushered in a House filled with lunatics in the 2010 election, and then doubled down in 2014!

Look around—all signs in our economy are up—and yet over two-thirds of our rank and file believe "we are moving in the wrong direction"—their perception is that our economy is in the tank—that we are in an economic malaise—a condition that would disappear overnight if we did, in fact, *Fix Unemployment*!

Best guess is that Congress passed, and President Obama signed into law HR 2847 [the HIRE Act], in 2009—which is based on fix the market, and this will fix unemployment [180 degrees off course]—but they did this because of the pervasive [but false] *belief* that "The market can provide anybody wanting a job, with a job"—it is *pure BS......it doesn't work*! Had we insisted on putting a lawnmower engine in the rocket to get us to the Moon....we would never have gotten there...[same difference]....and all of the empirical evidence is proof HR 2847 didn't create anywhere near the jobs needed...

Jim Green, Democrat opponent to Lamar Smith, Congress, 2000

CHAPTER EIGHTEEN

HOPPER-READY: THE NEIGHBOR-TO-NEIGHBOR JOB CREATION ACT

[1] PROPOSED LEGISLATION:

THE NEIGHBOR-TO-NEIGHBOR JOB CREATION ACT

A Pro-Market, deficit-neutral, federally mandated, Social Insurance, owned by our employed, to provide a fund to hire/train our unemployed.

SECTION 1. SHORT TITLE.

This Act shall be cited as The Neighbor-To-Neighbor Job Creation Act [To establish employment/training opportunities for the unemployed in compliance with the "Legal Authorization" in Public Law 15 USC § 3101, for the creation of a "reservoir of public employees", anytime our unemployment rate exceeds "3%", with an emphasis on training for market needs, including a training stipend, where there is a shortage of trained workers--hereafter NTN].

SEC. 2. DEFINITIONS.

In this Act the following definitions apply:

(1) SECRETARY- The term `Secretary' means the Secretary of Labor.

(2) STATE- The term `State' has the meaning given such term in section 102(2) of the Housing and Community Development Act (42 U.S.C. 5302(2)).

(3) TRUST FUND- The term `Trust Fund' refers to the Department of Labor Full Employment Trust Fund.

(4) UNIT OF GENERAL LOCAL GOVERNMENT- The term `unit of general local government' has the meaning given such term in section 102(1) of the Housing and Community Development Act (42 U.S.C. 5302(1)).

(5) URBAN COUNTY- The term `urban county' has the meaning given such term in section 102(6) of the Housing and Community Development Act (42 U.S.C. 5302(6)).

(6) WEB SITE- The Secretary shall establish an Internet Web site to serve as an information clearinghouse for job training and employment opportunities funded by the Trust Fund.

SEC. 3. EMPLOYMENT OPPORTUNITY GRANTS TO STATES, LOCAL GOVERNMENT.

(a) Use of Funds-A recipient of a grant under this section shall use the grant primarily for infrastructure repair, including, but not limited to:

(A) The painting and repair of schools, community centers, and libraries.
(B) The restoration and revitalization of abandoned and vacant properties to alleviate blight in distressed and foreclosure-affected areas of a unit of general local government.
(C) The augmentation of staffing in Head Start, child care, and other early childhood education programs to promote school readiness and early literacy.
(D) The renovation and enhancement of maintenance of parks, playgrounds, and other public spaces.

Respectfully Submitted,

Jim Green, Democrat candidate for Congress, Dist 21, TX, 2000

CHAPTER NINETEEN

WHAT WE NEED TO DO GOING FORWARD IN THE 21ST CENTURY:

Inexplicably "public employment" is seen the same as WPA—where millions are employed directly by the federal government—when that model is not only outmoded—it is insufficient to address our problems in the 21st century.

What we need today is an expanding and contracting public workforce—that expands during downturns in the market, and contracts as employees return to the private sector [Google: The Buffer Stock Employment Model]—triggered anytime our unemployment exceeds "3%" [as "authorized" under Humphrey-Hawkins]-- and least understood: This is an INDISPENSABLE component in the effective functioning of our 21st Century Market.

The market thrives when we have a robust, employed, consuming workforce—our manufacturers are sitting on $2 trillion in cash because they do not have consumers for their products—i.e., absent consumers, they lay off employees—[and the Republican solution, Reaganomics, has acted as an accelerate to this downward spiral—and which Romney promises to return us to if he is elected]!

In short, the above model is a "win-win" solution—the American people win, and capitalism wins!

To achieve this, what is being urged is "The Neighbor-To-Neighbor Job Creation Act": A federally mandated, mutual insurance—owned by our employed [from janitor to CEO] to create a fund to hire/train our unemployed.

To be viable, however, our job creation solution *MUST* contain:

1] Be based on the premise that we have far more work that needs to be done in America, than we have persons to fill these jobs.

2] It MUST have renewable funding.

3] It will not add a dime to our deficit.

To expand briefly, it is currently believed, erroneously, that we need "make work" jobs so that everyone who wants to work will have a job—but this is absurd—and an insult to "Yankee Ingenuity".

We do not have an unemployment crisis from a shortage of jobs, or money—but rather from a shortage of imagination.

Regarding "renewable funding" ALL of our job creation solutions, to date, have been based on the mind-set: "jump start" the market, and the market will in turn create all the jobs we need—and even setting aside that this is untrue, our current job creation is moving at a snail's pace—long past the unemployment benefits drying up—with the CBO projecting that even with the JOBS Act, signed into law on April 6, 2012--it will be 2017 before we return to a barely acceptable 5.5% unemployment rate!

Further, by its nature when we "jump start" --the employment ends when the funding runs out as we learned from the Stimulus—whereas any real fix to our unemployment crisis _demands_ renewable funding….

And whether the electorate will accept an unemployment rate hovering around 8% on election day—is the $64,000 question….

Regarding not adding a dime to our deficit—under The Neighbor-To-Neighbor Job Creation Act [NTN], the _funding_ to reduce our unemployment to 3% comes from an insurance owned by our employed, rather than added to our deficit—

If one is employed in America, participation in this insurance plan is mandatory—similar in concept to our auto insurance or Social Security Insurance [and without question the most successful social program in American history].

Jobs beget jobs--And with a modest policy cost of 4% of salary we can create more "private-sector" jobs in 6 months, that HR 2847, and the JOBS Act, in 6 years—and unlike these laws—NTN will not add a dime to our deficit!

Finally, this is in total concert with the will of the American people, i.e., that "anybody willing to work should be able to find a job"—and the American people have told our politicians time and again of their willingness to chip in to help their neighbor get a job [and as an *insurance*, as above, it also protects their continued employment]—it is just that Washington is deaf as an adder!

CHAPTER TWENTY

President Obama/Council of Economic Advisers:

Public-Sector jobs strengthen our free-enterprise market economy—i.e., they are a critical component to the viability of our 21st Century economy--rather than weakening the market--as propagandist, with one foot on the plantation, fraudulently deceive the public into believing for the purposes of exploiting American employees…..

Indeed, since WW II, the Koch brothers [both literally, and a metaphor, here, for the 1%] have spent tens of millions buying governors and legislators, to cement "at will" employment in every state [and currently only Montana limits to probationary employees]; and to destroy "collective bargaining", i.e., unions in America—

In sum, they have spent tens of millions of dollars to destroy "employee rights" in America!

To understand the importance of "collective bargaining" for employees, it is informative to take a page from history:

When Hitler became the dictator in Germany, one of his first laws was to make it illegal for more than three persons to gather on the street—and German citizens were subject to immediate arrest if they did.

The same principal is being used by preventing employees putting their heads together, as it were, to bargain for employee rights—and recently one group of employees placed "job security" over a salary increase—with the irony being that the specific objective of "at will" employment—is to destroy "job security"!

In short, the deceptive propaganda to frighten Americans regarding "public-sector" jobs, has but a single parent: To exploit American labor—by some, to assuage deep-seated feelings of inferiority [they can only feel tall, by making others small, in their eyes]-—but most often for just pure GREED!

Where our policies makers go wrong by pandering to some in the oligarchy—and/or buying into this fraudulent propaganda:

Unemployment is a NO ONE WINS—the jobless lose, civility loses, and the market loses, to wit:

THE LAW OF DIMINISHED INCOME TO THE MARKET FROM UNEMPLOYMENT [hereafter D/UE LAW]

Short Definition:

> 3% is the zero-sum threshold above which unemployment starts substantially undermining the Market--and the loss in income to the Market is compounded exponentially with each

percentage point of increase in unemployment, above 3%.

Ref: IT IS IMPOSSIBLE TO BE A CHRISTIAN, AND VOTE REPUBLICAN, Amazon

Jim Green, Democrat opponent to Lamar Smith, 2000

CHAPTER TWENTY-ONE

FAIL-SAFE ELECTRONIC VOTING

TO THE READER: Given you have gotten this far, and agree with the proposed changes—and particularly given the pernicious Citizens United—our democracy, and the above, or any, progress, will be in peril absent a "fail-safe" electronic voting system. The following is my proposed solution, and like every solution proposed, here, feed-back--your proposed improvement, etc. is welcomed:

THE FAIL-SAFE ELECTRONIC VOTING ACT

1) EVERY electronic voting machine (hereafter EVM), must be inexpensive, identical throughout the U.S. in a 1/150 ratio, and *must count and produce a hard-copy of the recorded votes.* In addition, an extra copy of their recorded votes would be produced (not necessarily a hard-copy), marked "Voter's Copy", and containing "NOTICE: Do Not Destroy Until Every Election On Your Ballot Is Certified". [If Wal-Mart handed us a piece of paper with the words "trust us" as a receipt for our purchases—we would be outraged—and yet, this is our current electronic voting nightmare—but in this case it is our democracy at risk]!

2) *After confirming that their votes are recorded correctly*, the voter would then insert the hard-copy ballot into a software-free (count only) optical scanner (hereafter OS), for a second count. The hard-copy

ballot would be retained by election officials in the event a candidate asks for a recount (*not possible under the current system, and which undermines the legality of each such election*). The EVM and the OS must be manufactured by different companies (which is universally true today).

3) Election officials assigned to oversee the EVM, would be prevented by law from overseeing the OS, and vice-versa, and stiff criminal penalties would be imposed for violations.

4) Further, every EVM would be programmed with raw data re the total registration rolls, by party, and norms for their voting history, etc.,----as an "alert" to a possible irregularity, such as an "under-vote"—or "vote-flipping" etc., and *standards* established to suspend certification where there is an "improbable result", at least temporarily, of a particular election until the discrepancy is cleared up. (This is what computers do best, and it would be very easy to create such a program).

5) At the end of the election day, tallies would be taken from the EVM and the OS, for each candidate. *If the tallies didn't balance for any given election, or if there is an "alert", that election cannot be certified until the "error" is corrected.* If the candidates agree (the victory is certain), minor discrepancies in the count could be disregarded. While probably rare, the Voter, or a random sample of Voters, would be required by law to return their Copy of the recorded votes to the election

office to clear up any "error", or where an "alert" signals the need for same.

6) Further, every state provides for a recount when the total vote falls below a certain percent of difference between the candidates, impossible to conduct with the current EVM. And thus Congress must mandate the following regarding presidential candidates: A RUN-OFF election is mandated and triggered in those states where the percent of total vote is less than .5% of difference between the two candidates; said election to be held on the second Saturday following the election, on PAPER BALLOTS ONLY, and contain ONLY the names of the relevant candidates, for instance: "Barack Obama, Democrat" and "John McCain, Republican"—with oversight in counting by a representative(s) of each party—said procedure providing more than adequate time to meet the Electoral College mandate [Ideally, all of this could be eliminated if we did away with the Electoral College, but until then....]. NOTE: Had this been the law in 2000, Al Gore would be our president, and America would have been spared the economic, etc., disaster that followed!

7) Finally, absent the above safeguards, and until these safeguards are in place--Congress must mandate that PAPER BALLOTS, ONLY, can be used in our presidential elections. This is not a "partisan" issue, it is a "pro-democracy" issue. Most importantly, this will return the responsibility for our elections, and our vote counting, back into the hands of the individual voter, where it belongs, and out of the hands of "corporate control"---*it is after all "our democracy", itself, that is at*

risk if we don't take these steps---and in that regard, is there any time or cost differential that is too great?

Jim Green

CHAPTER TWENTY-TWO

I didn't write the following. It is a cut and paste from **FACEBOOK,** or some blog [would like to give credit if knew the author]--but it is so on target regarding how "fear" is driving Conservative policy in America today—i.e., is undermining America and our progress—and relegating America to a Third World country status, rather than a world leader—FDR had it on the nose in "All we have to fear, is fear itself"…at his inaugural in 1933….

"Conservatives are such cowards: they are afraid of gay people getting married or serving in the military; they are afraid of bringing terrorists to super max prisons in the US from which no one has ever escaped; they are afraid of the boy scouts letting gay kids in; they are afraid of everyone voting and are constantly suppressing the vote under some bogus voter fraud theory; they are afraid of letting students vote at their universities; they are afraid of women having the right to choose; they even are afraid of women getting contraception [the real issue actually is a women's agency and control over their bodies]; they are afraid of immigration reform leading to citizenship because they are afraid of-- name whatever reason; they are afraid of mandating gun purchasers to undergo background checks for crazy people and terrorists; they are afraid of people smoking pot; they are afraid of climate change being real and contradicting their beloved Bible; they are afraid of legitimate campaign reform; they are afraid of Muslims; they are afraid of blacks; they are afraid of atheists; they are afraid of hippies; they are afraid of socialists; they are probably still afraid of monsters under their beds; they are just rank cowards and keep making things up to be afraid of."

CHAPTER TWENTY-THREE

[I couldn't resist including this...and yes I am the author.....]

A MESSAGE FROM GOD

MANY CENTURIES AGO, a man of the cloth, we don't know his name, and in a flash of insight (perhaps induced by peyote) told his flock that "sex is a sin". And lo and behold he learned that by taking a very natural and healthy part of our life and turning it into something that was "dirty and nasty", that he could imprison his flock, and fill his coffers, and hallelujah it was a great day for the Lord!

Quickly, his miracle spread to other churches in his village, and then to the next village, and then the next county, and then state, and soon it spread to all the churches in the ancient world, and all of their flocks cowed in fear and shame and became imprisoned, and their coffers over-floweth. Hallelujah, it was a great day for the Lord!

And to keep the myth alive they started inventing stories, half-baked stories, that made no sense to anyone who is rational, such as "Mary was a virgin"— well, she just had to be a virgin because she would never partake in anything that was dirty and nasty, like sex (if you're doing it right), and this was necessary to make "sex is a sin" make sense...so they invented a Mary that was "sinless"--you get the picture. And their coffers over-floweth. Hallelujah, it was a great day for the Lord!

No one seemed to be bothered that when we play tricks on the human mind by taking something that is very natural and healthy, such as sex, and make it dirty and nasty that all kinds of bad things happen to the human mind:

Such as most pedophiles, and most serial killers, and voting Republican, and unwarranted suicides, and most mental illness, and unwanted pregnancies. (Teens not wanting to have sex is the perversion, not the other way around, and by replacing sex education and condoms, with unrealistic "abstinence", and by using blather about "low self-esteem" to shame them into not "sinning"—We have a teen pregnancy in the U.S. twice that of England and Canada!).

But none of this mattered, because their coffers over-floweth, and Hallelujah, it is a great day for the Lord!

There is a cure--------Tell our right-wing hypocrites, who Judge, rather than "Judge not".... to shove it....

GOD

ABOUT THE AUTHOR: I was employed in our Criminal Justice System for a cumulative 20 years as a probation officer, with 5 of those years as a chief probation officer. I authored the concept of "Shock Incarceration" which became law in Kansas in 1970, and then was adopted in numerous jurisdictions in the U.S. and also spread to Europe—it is currently identified in the U.S. as "Boot Camp" [as the means to "shock" the young offender—and a total distortion of my original intent—like many ideas, once released, they take on a life of their own]. I also instigated establishment of the first Court Psychiatric Clinic in the U.S., in conjunction with psychiatrists from the Menninger Foundation, as a chief probation officer. Finally, I was the Democrat candidate for Congress, District 21, TX, 2000. I would most define myself as a Social Ecologist-- [albeit my degree is in Psychology]. My web page is www.Inclusivism.org –which has been on the internet since 1996.
http://www.amazon.com/James-L.-Jim-Green/e/B001KHZIMM/ref=ntt_dp_epwbk_0

\

A BRIEF ADDENDUM: When the U.S. Supreme Court denied certiorari—where the violation of my constitutional rights were obvious, and criminal negligence on the part of the government defendants in the death of our son, equally obvious—[detailed in THE HARVARD BOYS CLUB, Amazon/Kindle]--I filed a Petition for Rehearing [which is automatic]—and included the following. The Clerk of the U.S. Supreme Court called me at my work in California, and asked that I withdraw the "cartoon" [a reprint from The NEW YORKER] from my Petition. I refused on the basis of the First Amendment, and it remains in the archives at the U.S. Supreme Court [Docket #: 79-1627], to this day. The wording [not that clear] is: "Excellent, excellent. A fine blend of truths, half-truths, and blatant falsehoods".

IN THE

Supreme Court of the United States

October Term, 1979

No. 79-1627

JAMES L. GREEN,

Petitioner,

vs.

"Excellent, excellent. A fine blend of truths, half-truths, and blatant falsehoods."

www.ingramcontent.com/pod-product-compliance
Lightning Source LLC
Chambersburg PA
CBHW050508290526
45786CB00006B/2481